GEARED FOR GROWTH BIBLE STUDIES

THE MAKER'S INSTRUCTIONS

A STUDY IN PROVERBS

BIBLE STUDIES TO IMPACT THE LIVES
OF ORDINARY PEOPLE

Written By Shirley Andrews

The Word Worldwide

CHRISTIAN
FOCUS

For details of our titles visit us on our website
www.christianfocus.com

ISBN 978-1-78191-970-5

Copyright © WEC International

Published in 2017
by
Christian Focus Publications Ltd.,
Geanies House, Fearn, Ross-shire,
IV20 1TW, Scotland, UK,
and
WEC International, Bulstrode, Oxford Road,
Gerrards Cross, Bucks, SL9 8SZ.

Cover design by Alister MacInnes

Printed in the UK by Bell & Bain, Glasgow.

MIX
Paper from
responsible sources
FSC® C007785
www.fsc.org

CONTENTS

QUESTIONS AND NOTES

ANSWER GUIDE

PREFACE

GEARED FOR GROWTH

Where there's LIFE there's GROWTH:
Where there's GROWTH there's LIFE.

WHY GROW a study group?
Because as we study and share the Bible together we can

- learn to combat loneliness, depression, staleness, frustration and other problems
- get to understand and love each other
- become responsive to the Holy Spirit's dealing and obedient to God's Word *and that's GROWTH.*

How do you GROW a study group?

- Just by asking a friend to join you and then aim at expanding your group
- Study the set portions daily (they are brief and easy: no catches)
- Meet once a week to discuss what you find
- Befriend others, both Christians and non-Christians, and work away together

see how it GROWS!

WHEN you GROW ...

This will happen at school, at home, at work, in your youth group, your student fellowship, women's meetings, mid-week meetings, churches and communities, and so on.

you'll be REACHING THROUGH TEACHING

WHEN you PRAY ...

Remember those involved in the writing and production of the study courses: pray for missionaries and nationals working on the translations into many different languages. Pray for groups studying that each member will not only be enriched personally, but will be reaching out continually to involve others. Pray for group leaders and those who direct the studies locally, nationally and internationally.

WHEN you PRAY ... Realise that all profits from sales of studies go to develop the ministry on our mission fields and beyond, pay translators, and so on, and have the joy of knowing you are working together with them in the task.

INTRODUCTORY STUDY

GOD'S WISDOM FOR LIVING

Most people begin to hear proverbs as children in their home. In our home my grandmother, great-aunt and mother used many proverbs. Did you hear proverbs such as 'Too many cooks spoil the broth' and 'A stitch in time saves nine?'

WHAT IS A PROVERB?

- It is a short and often wise saying that sums up a truth in a few words.
- Proverbs are practical, to do with daily living.
- Proverbs are often thought-provoking and easy to remember.
- Proverbs are crystallised truth – crystallised wisdom.

WHAT'S YOUR PROVERB?

Working in twos or as individuals, think of a proverb and then share it with the group.

WHAT IS THE BOOK OF PROVERBS?

People all over the world in all ages have used proverbs. In ancient times people had collections of proverbs. In those times few people could read, but by using proverbs they had the crystallised wisdom of their fathers.

The Old Testament people of God had their collection of Proverbs also.

The Bible is made up of sixty-six books. These sixty-six books are of different kinds. Some of the books are history that tell the story of individuals, nations and especially of God's people, the nation of Israel. Some books are letters to individuals and to churches. Four books are gospels that tell the story of Jesus, His birth, life and ministry, death and resurrection. Some books are books of the law.

'Proverbs' is an Old Testament book that is part of the wisdom books in the Bible. The wisdom books are Job, Proverbs and Ecclesiastes. Proverbs is made up of wise sayings and short teachings or sermons – God's wisdom for living life…

WHAT ARE SOME OF THE LIFE ISSUES IN PROVERBS?

11:1	11:22	12:9	12:15
12:16	12:18	12:28	14:1
14:30	15:17	17:22	25:12
25:19	29:15	29:20	

In Proverbs we have God's wisdom for living our daily lives.

'I find my microwave oven a very useful appliance in the kitchen. From time to time I need to get out the maker's instructions to learn how to use my microwave and care for it. I follow the directions for cooking times and the cleaning instructions. I heed the warnings that I could damage it by using any metal containers and by operating the microwave without anything in it. A friend bought a sophisticated and expensive microwave. One night her husband was minding the children and he knew his wife used the microwave to heat the baby's bottle. He felt that he did not need to read instructions.

So he put the bottle in, teat and all, pressed the buttons and went off to do something else. An hour later the timer rang. His wife came home to a melted mess in her microwave.

Some people live their lives like this. They feel that they do not need to know the Maker's instructions. They get their lives in a great mess. Proverbs is a book of our Maker's practical instructions on how to live the life He has given us.

WHAT ARE SOME OF THE LIFE ISSUES IN PROVERBS?

Read Proverbs 1:1-7.

From these verses write at least two things by which you personally may expect to profit by studying this book:

1. ....

2. ....

Share these as a group.

In the prayer time you could ask the Lord to build you up in these two things in your life. Or you could pray for one another about these matters.

NOTES

Quotes from the Bible in this study are mostly from the New International Version. I find the Tyndale Bible Commentary on *Proverbs* by Derek Kidner a great blessing, and often quote from it in this study.

As Proverbs is a collection of sometimes unconnected truths, our study will jump from place to place in the book. So make it a goal to read through the book over the next ten weeks at least once, preferably several times.

STUDY 1

WISDOM IS SKILL IN LIVING LIFE

QUESTIONS

DAY 1 *Proverbs 1:1-7*
a) What is the purpose of Proverbs? You should find at least seven purposes in verses 1-6.

b) What indication is there in verse 3 that this is meant to be a very practical book?

DAY 2 *Proverbs 1:7-19.*
a) Write down the motto of the book (Prov. 1:7).

b) From verses 8-9 whose teaching is the son to hear?

c) How is this father helping his son deal with the enticement of his peers?

DAY 3 *Proverbs 1:1; 25:1.*
a) Who was the chief writer of Proverbs?

b) Proverbs 22:17: What does this verse tell us about the writers of Proverbs 22:17 to 24:34?

c) Proverbs 30:1; 31:1: Who is responsible for the writing of the last two chapters of Proverbs?

DAY 4 *2 Chronicles 1:7-13.*
a) God said to Solomon, 'Ask for whatever you want me to give you'. What was Solomon's choice and why did he choose that way?

b) What other things could he have chosen?

DAY 5   *I Kings 4:29-34.*
a) How did God respond to Solomon's request for wisdom?

b) Proverbs 2:6, 10, and 3:13. How may you expect God to answer your request to give you wisdom?

DAY 6   *Proverbs 1:20-33.*
Sometimes Proverbs personifies wisdom as a woman. The woman, 'Wisdom' walks about.
a) From verses 20-21, what significance do you see in the places that Wisdom was walking?

b) From verses 22-33 to whom was she calling, what was she offering and what was the response of the people?

c) How does verse 29 still apply to people today?

DAY 7   *Proverbs 3:29-35.*
a) From verse 35, what are the two groups that make up mankind, and what contrast is made between these two groups?

b) Matthew 7:24-27. What contrasts does Jesus make in His story of the wise man and the fool?

NOTES

THE KEY WORD IN PROVERBS IS 'WISDOM'

This book is God's wisdom applied to the many facets of life, e.g. 'A gentle answer turns away wrath, but a harsh word stirs up anger' (Prov. 15:1). This is God's wisdom about how best to reply to an insult or a mean word. To answer like the proverb suggests, to give a gentle answer, would keep us out of much trouble and pain.

God very much wants you to know how to live. He cares very much about the kind of life you live. He cares about the way you live with your family. If you are married He cares about the way you live with your husband or wife and children. He cares about the way you live with your friends and neighbours, at your work and in business. He cares about the way you do His work. He cares about your words and the way you speak. In Proverbs God teaches us about all these matters. He wants you to be wise.

The biblical understanding of wisdom is not just knowing truth, but living truth. A person may know much but may not be very wise at all! Have you found this to be so?

PROVERBS CONSISTS OF SHORT TEACHINGS AND WISE SAYINGS

In Proverbs 1:10-19, we read the short teaching the father gave his son. Proverbs consists of short teachings like this, together with many short, wise sayings, like Proverbs 15:1. The whole of the book of Proverbs speaks about wisdom.

THE OLD TESTAMENT WORD FOR WISDOM MEANS: SKILL AT LIVING LIFE

In Proverbs we will learn of the value of wisdom, the many kinds of blessings wisdom brings, how to get wisdom, and the consequences of not choosing wisdom.

Ruth is a very able woman. She was very able in her profession, and has leadership, administrative and teaching skills. But she also knows the way of wisdom. She is wise in the care of her family. She is very wise in the matter of relationships. She is wise in her words. She is wise with her money. She is wise in doing God's work. She is wise in the church. Many people go to her to get help for their lives. They recognise that she has wisdom – skill in living life. Her life is a great blessing. Do you know someone like her?

PROVERBS TEACHES ABOUT THE WISE AND THE FOOLS

But not everyone in the world is like Ruth. She is one of what Proverbs calls 'the wise'. Proverbs sees the whole of mankind in one of two groups – the wise and fools. Sometimes fools are called 'the wicked', 'the simple', 'the scoffers', 'mockers'. The wise are sometimes called 'the righteous', 'the upright.'

All through Proverbs all kinds of contrasts are made between the wise and the fools, e.g. Proverbs 12:15, 'The way of a fool seems right to him, but a wise man listens to advice.

Proverbs 15:29, 'The LORD is far from the wicked but He hears the prayer of the righteous.'

The righteous do what is right in God's eyes. Fools choose to go their own way and like doing that. The simple are deceived and walk in wrong ways. Scoffers make fun of the things of God.

Without a mirror can a man see his own ears? It has been said that a fool can no more see his own folly than he can see his own ears.

As we study Proverbs it is important to see what God says a fool is and does. In that way we can avoid being fools ourselves.

Do you want the Lord to show you the things in your life that fools do? What will you do about these things?

STUDY 2

CHOOSE THE WAY OF WISDOM

QUESTIONS

DAY 1   *Proverbs 2:1-22.*
(Before you do today's study read the first page of the notes).
a) What are some of the other words for wisdom used in these verses?

b) From this chapter, what are some of the blessings of getting wisdom, of walking in the way of the wise?

DAY 2   *Proverbs 2:1-22.*
a) What do verses 1-5 say about the level of commitment needed to get wisdom?

b) What do verses 7, 8, 9, 12, 13, 15, 19, 20 tell us about ways and paths.

DAY 3   *Proverbs 9:4-12.*
a) Write down the motto of Proverbs, given in verse 10. What does this verse tell us about the fear of the Lord?

b) What are some bad kinds of fears and what do they bring to our lives?

c) What are some helpful kinds of fears and what do they bring to our lives?

DAY 4   *Proverbs 14:26-27; 19:23; 22:4; 31:30.*
a) Why is the fear of the Lord a great blessing for your life?

b) Proverbs 1:29. What does the fool do about the fear of the Lord?

QUESTIONS (contd)

DAY 5   *Proverbs 8:1-13.*

a) What claims does Wisdom make about her words and the value of her instruction?

b) From verses 7 and 13, write what Wisdom hates.

DAY 6   *Proverbs 6:16 -19; 15:26; 16:5*

a) What do these verses tell us as to what God hates and the things He loves?

b) Proverbs 8:13. Write down the first part of the verse. What does this verse tell us about the attitude of the wise to all kinds of sin?

DAY 7   *Proverbs 16:6; 23:17-18.*

a) Why is the fear of the Lord very desirable for your life and a great blessing?

b) The following are true examples:

Harriet claims to be a Christian, filled with the Spirit. She continually lies very skilfully. She misrepresents situations. She deceives her husband. She does not seem to find lying a problem.

Damien and Lindy are Christian leaders of the youth group. They are living in sexual immorality. They have no sense that this is out of order. They do not see that it presents a problem as far as their example to the youth is concerned.

Don is the rector's warden, vocal and influential in a well-known church. Just before the visit of the bishop the prison chaplain rang

QUESTIONS (contd)

the amazed, and totally unsuspecting rector to tell him Don was facing trial that week for embezzling £250,000 over the previous five years, with the possibility of five years in jail.

   i) What do you think is missing in these Christians' lives?

   ii) Think about your life. Do you have a sin you keep on doing? Do you hate that sin? What changes would there be in your life if you had the fear of the Lord?

NOTES

We can liken the concept of wisdom to a rainbow. A rainbow is made up of different colours. In the same way there are many things included in the concept of wisdom. Some helpful thoughts from Derek Kidner's commentary on Proverbs:

'In chapter 1:1-7, Proverbs opens by breaking up the plain daylight of wisdom into its constituent colours. These all shade into one another, and any of them can be used to represent the whole; yet there is some value in seeing them grouped together.

1 *Instruction or training* – giving notice that wisdom will be hard won, a quality of character as much of mind. Its frequent companion is correction or reproof. These two terms can be summed up as discipline, they give the reminder that wisdom is not to be had through extra-mural study: it is for disciples only.

2 *Understanding or insight.* The background verb to these words is 'discern'.

3 *Wise dealing* – i.e. good sense, practical wisdom. In its verb form it means 'to be successful.'

4 *Shrewdness and discretion* – the power of forming plans.

5 *Knowledge* – not so much an informed mind but a knowing of truth and of God Himself, learning – emphasises that truth is something given and received, or grasped.

So instruction, training, understanding, insight, wise dealing, discretion, knowledge are all part of wisdom.'

Proverbs declares that all mankind falls into one of two groups: the wise and fools. Proverbs declares that all mankind are walking in one of two ways: the way of the wise and the way of fools.

You walk in the way of wisdom or the way of the wicked.

A MAIN THEME OF PROVERBS IS THE FEAR OF THE LORD.

Fear is a very powerful emotion. Some people fear getting sick, having accidents, death, other people, bad things happening to their children, Friday 13th, cancer and many other things. Such fears cripple our lives and take away our peace and joy. I fear snakes, spiders, speeding in the car, thieves, faulty electrical things and swimming in polluted water. These are helpful fears. I know these things can do me much harm. Because I fear these things I stay away from them.

Many times in the Old Testament the Lord said to His people, 'Fear not.' Jesus said many times to His disciples, 'Fear not.'

THE FEAR OF THE LORD IS THE BEGINNING OF WISDOM

The fear of the Lord is like the foundation of a house. The fear of the Lord is the foundation on which wisdom is built. It is good to be right with the Lord, to be in awe of Him and worship Him.

Proverbs 8:13a tells us this about the fear of the Lord:

'To fear the LORD is to hate evil.'

Something to make: You could print these two verses about the fear of the Lord on some card, put them above the sink, on the fridge or a helpful place for you. They are key verses in Proverbs.

God tells us, His children, the things that He hates and the things that He loves.

WISDOM IS SEEING EVIL AS GOD SEES IT

But the fear of the Lord is a choice. Fools do not choose the fear of the Lord. **The fear of the LORD – it's your choice.**

STUDY 3

THE BLESSING OF GETTING WISDOM

QUESTIONS

DAY 1   *Proverbs 3:1 – 8.*

a) In verse 6 God tells us one of the blessings of getting wisdom is that He will make our paths straight. What conditions are there for you to receive this blessing?

b) What does the picture of God making 'your paths straight' mean to you?

c) Who are you to trust with all your heart? Who are you to fear? How does that trust and fear go together?

DAY 2   *Proverbs 3:13-26.*

a) From these verses list the blessings of getting wisdom.

b) Do you desire for your life the outworking of wisdom described in Proverbs 3:21-26? Why?

DAY 3   *Proverbs 2:12-16; 4:6.*

a) In what ways does wisdom offer us protection?

b) Where do you meet up with crooked and perverse people?

DAY 4   *Proverbs 6:20-35.*

a) What explanation is given as to how God's wisdom protects us?

b) What example are we given of how God's wisdom is a great protection?

QUESTIONS (contd)

DAY 5 *Wisdom's Feast Proverbs 9:1-12.*
Wisdom and Folly invite all people to the feast they each prepare.
a) What preparations does Wisdom make for her feast and who does she invite?

b) What does she offer and what does she require?

DAY 6 *Folly's Feast Proverbs 9:13-18.*
a) What description is given of Folly?

b) What do you see about the invitation of Wisdom (v. 4) and that of Folly (v. 16).

c) What does she offer and what is the outcome for her guests?

DAY 7 *Proverbs 2:6*
What does the father tell his son about where to get wisdom?
Proverbs 4:1-9; 8:17.

NOTES

One of the truths repeated again and again in Proverbs is that to get wisdom, to walk in wisdom, brings many kinds of blessing. Those who walk in God's ways are given the very best life.

Proverbs chapters 2 and 3 tell us of many of the blessings of walking in wisdom. We read of life, favour and a good name in the sight of God and man, health, wholeness and nourishment to our inner being. The blessings of life and peace come from walking in wisdom.

Think of the way of the wicked. I know a father of four young sons. He has been binge-drinking for twenty years. He is only forty and his liver is now destroyed. Drinking with friends is fun, was very pleasurable but it has not led to life for him or for his family!

THE BLESSING OF STRAIGHT PATHS

Proverbs 3:5-6 are some of the well-known verses from Proverbs. Maybe you learned them at Sunday School.

Something to make: You could print these two verses on some card, put them with the two verses from week 2 above the sink, on the fridge, or a helpful place for you. They are key verses in Proverbs.

'Trust in the Lord with all your heart and lean not on your own understanding; in all your ways acknowledge him, and he will make your paths straight.'

Have you already memorised these verses? If you have not done so they are worth memorising!

WISDOM IS NOT LEANING ON YOUR OWN UNDERSTANDING

All around us there are people longing for peace, that deep inner peace. Many take sedatives, others take illegal drugs, while others use alcohol to get peace. These are the things Folly offers.

We hear this about the ways of Wisdom: 'Her ways are pleasant ways and all her paths are peace', (3:17). Walking in wisdom helps us with those wrong fears that destroy. Proverbs 3:26 says, 'For the Lord will be your confidence and will keep your foot from being snared.

In his commentary on Proverbs 3:21-26, Kidner says, 'It becomes clear that wisdom means walking with God' (vv. 23-26).

Another of the good blessings of getting wisdom is the protection she gives. Proverbs tells us the truth about sin. It tells the truth about adultery.

WISDOM PROTECTS US FROM WICKED MEN AND WOMEN

All through Proverbs contrasts are made. As wisdom is personified as a woman, 'Wisdom', so foolishness is personified as a woman, 'Folly'. Proverbs chapter 9 tells us that all people get invitations to two different feasts. For your life there are:

TWO INVITATIONS, TWO FEASTS

Both Wisdom and Folly seem to offer the same thing. Both say, 'Whoever is simple, let him turn in here!' Wisdom offers life. But all people die who eat the feast Folly prepares. Folly tells us 'Stolen water is sweet, and bread eaten in secret is pleasant.' Folly tells us for a man to lie with a woman not his wife is sweet. Folly tells us to steal money and use it is sweet. Folly tells us gossip is sweet. Folly tells us that all kinds of sins are sweet. Folly tells people that they can enjoy sin. And they do. People enjoy sin for a time. It is true that often sin is sweet. But folly never tells the whole truth. It is like eating some foods that taste good. But when you wake up next day you have a bad taste in your mouth. Proverbs 20:17 says, 'Food gained by fraud tastes sweet to a man but he ends up with a mouth full of gravel.'

Have you accepted the invitation of wisdom?

Maybe in your group you could think of at least ten blessings you have in your life because you have accepted the invitation of Wisdom.

And the good news is **that wisdom is a free gift and that wisdom is for all that look for it, and for all who ask for it.**

It's your choice. Do you want to look for wisdom? Do you want to ask for wisdom?

STUDY 4

GOD'S WISDOM ON THE TONGUE

QUESTIONS

DAY 1 *Proverbs 10:11-14, 18-21, 31-32.*
a) From these verses how is the tongue and speech used by the wise and the fool?

b) Verse 21 tells us, 'the lips of the righteous nourish many.' How do we do that?

DAY 2 *Proverbs 11:9; 18:4-8, 20-21; 20:15.*
a) What do you learn from these verses about the power of the tongue and the value of words?

b) What does Proverbs 18:21 tell you about the power of words?

DAY 3 *Proverbs 18:21*
a) How do you feel that your words can speak life to others?

b) In a Year 9 RE class I met Dean. He was demoralised, discouraged, disinterested and not doing well at school but he was interested in RE. He told me that when he was only nine years old his teacher told the class, 'Dean is dumb!' In what ways did that teacher's words bring death to Dean?

DAY 4 *Proverbs 12:6; 15:1-4; 16:23-27.*
a) What contrasts do you see between the tongue of the wise and the tongue of fools?

b) What wonderful thing do you see about the tongue of the wise, repeated in 15:4 and 16:24?

QUESTIONS (contd)

c) How do you think your tongue can be used for healing?

DAY 5 *Proverbs 6:16-19.*
a) What are the things about the tongue that God hates?

Proverbs 12:19-22; 13:5; 19:5, 9; 26:28.
b) What do you learn about truthful lips, lies and lying lips?

c) What about exaggeration, half-truths and 'white lies'?

DAY 6 *Proverbs 11:13; 17:9; 20:19.*
a) All of us are told things in confidence by other people. What does Proverbs tell us about confidences?

Proverbs 11:13; 17:4,9; 18:8; 20:19; 26:20-22.
b) Betraying confidences and gossip go hand in hand. What is gossip like and what does it do?

c) What are you to do about gossip and those who gossip?

DAY 7 *Proverbs 19:13; 21:9, 19; 25:24; 27:15-16.*
a) Men and women, young and old nag. What effect does nagging have on a home? How do you break the nagging habit?

Proverbs 27:1-2.
b) What is God's wisdom about boasting?

NOTES

In her marriage preparation a friend was told that there were three things that couples fight about most: words, money and sex.

God knows us well! These are key areas in each of our lives. And these are the three areas about which God gives us much teaching in Proverbs. Each one of these areas has the potential to be of great blessing to us or of great destruction. For the next three weeks we will spend a week on each of these three key areas. We begin this week on the tongue. It is such a small part of the body but it is capable of doing great things, both good and evil. Proverbs teaches us that our words are important.

THE WISE PERSON KNOWS THE VALUE OF WORDS

Proverbs gives us some beautiful pictures of the tongue of the wise. Their tongue is a fountain of life, it is choice silver, a tree of life, like sweet honeycomb, sweet to the soul and healing to the bones. Your tongue has marvellous potential!

THE MOUTH OF THE RIGHTEOUS IS A FOUNTAIN OF LIFE

The mouth of a wise person is like a spring of clean, good water. In Kenya there is a huge spring, Mzima Springs, in the middle of a parched, barren desert. Very little grows in the area. But in the middle of that desert a spring of pure, sweet water comes up out of the ground. From this spring a river flows, the water supply for Mombasa. Fish, hippopotamus and crocodiles live in the river. By the river everything is lush and huge trees grow.

THE TONGUE HAS THE POWER OF LIFE AND DEATH

Proverbs also gives us some fearful pictures of the tongue – like thrusts of a sword or a scorching fire. Our words can be like a thrust of a sword to another's heart. Swords are designed to wound and to bring death. Words are capable of doing just that. Often a child carries the wound of words for years and their lives are often controlled by those words. At school a friend of mine was constantly called 'Opium, a slow-moving dope.' His life could easily have been controlled by these words that were not true. Another friend was told by her mother, 'You are no good. You never will be any good. You are not like your sister.' Even now in middle age she still struggles to live free of these words.

> Our words have great value because they have great power.
> They have the power to bring life or power to bring death.
> They have the power to rescue or power to destroy.
> They have the power to heal or power to wound.

Think about your life.

Think of some kind, life-giving words that have been said to you. Who said them?

How did these words bless your life?

Think about some cutting, hurtful accusing, mocking words that have been said to you. What did they bring to your life? (Healing comes by forgiving the other person. But sometimes the power of spoken words needs to be broken in our lives also).

Think about your tongue:

MY TONGUE – A TREE OF LIFE OR A SCORCHING FIRE?

The tongue of the wise brings healing. Words have the power to bring healing to others. Aspirin is a good medicine. It helps us when we have fever, toothache, headache, earache and minor injuries. Aspirin brings healing for pain of many kinds. As good medicine can bring healing, so words can bring healing to others. Do you know someone whose tongue is a fountain of life, a tree of life, a tongue that brings healing?

We sometimes have to speak words of rebuke or correction. The wise person never says such words when they are angry. Words of rebuke and correction can be of great blessing. But sometimes words like that, although true, can wound deeply. Ephesians 4:15 tells us the answer to this problem. We must always 'speak the truth in love.'

THE SPEECH OF THE WISE IS TRUE AND NOT FALSE

Proverbs warns us about habits we can fall into with our tongues like lying, gossiping, nagging, bragging and flattering. People who complain and nag often want to quarrel, fight with words. They find fault with what others do. In Proverbs we read of a wife that nags. But men nag and children also!

Proverbs 19:13 (GNT) 'A nagging wife is like water going drip-drip-drip.'

Are you ever tempted to lie, tell secrets, gossip, nag or brag? Only you can answer that question. King David knew he needed God's help to have the tongue of a wise man. This is one of David's prayers for his tongue: 'Set a guard over my mouth, O Lord, keep watch over the door of my lips!' (Ps. 141:3).

Write a prayer for your mouth and the way you want to use your tongue. You may want to use these prayers in the group.

STUDY 5

WISDOM ABOUT WEALTH

QUESTIONS

DAY 1 *1 Corinthians 3:18-20.*
a) What does Paul tell us about being wise and the two kinds of wisdom?

b) In the media we get much wisdom of the world about money and wealth. What are some of the messages you hear?

DAY 2 *Proverbs 15:16-17; 16:8; 17:1.*
a) What contrasts are made between much money and wealth and spiritual blessings?

b) What is of greater value and what are better choices?

DAY 3 *Proverbs 11:4, 28; 23:4-5; 27:23-24.*
a) What does wisdom tell us about the danger, and the lasting value of money and wealth?

b) What happens when Christians lose sight of these truths about money and wealth?

Proverbs 24:3-4.
c) What beautiful picture is given of the life of someone who walks in wisdom?

DAY 4 *Proverbs 14:20-24; 31; 19:17; 22:9; 28:27.*
a) In what important way are we to use money and wealth to honour the Lord, and what blessing is promised if we do so?

QUESTIONS (contd)

b) Who do you regard as poor?

DAY 5 *Proverbs 3:5-10.*
a) What other vital way are we, urban Christians today, to honour the Lord with our wealth and what blessing is promised if we do so?

b) How do verses 9-10 tie in with trusting God and acknowledging Him in all our ways?

DAY 6 *Proverbs 17:8, 23; 18:16; 29:4.*
a) Why is the giving of bribes, or big 'gifts' destructive personally and nationally?

Proverbs 11:1; 16:11; 20:10,23.
b) What is the Lord looking for in our lives in the handling of money and wealth?

DAY 7 *Proverbs 30:7 – 9.*
a) How much money and wealth did this wise man ask the Lord to give him?

Why did he pray that way?

Proverbs 10:22.
b) Where can you find true riches and lasting wealth?

NOTES

This week we study the wisdom God gives us about money and wealth and His wisdom as to how to handle it. Money and wealth can be of tremendous blessing or a great snare for our lives.

MONEY AND WEALTH ARE GOOD GIFTS FROM GOD

God is the Giver of all good things. He places money and wealth in our care. But we need to know and follow God's wisdom in handling money and wealth, or it can shipwreck our faith.

Along with God's wisdom, Christians are surrounded by another kind of wisdom, the wisdom of the world. Every day we hear the wisdom of the world about money and wealth, things like: 'Money and wealth will bring you true happiness. How much money and wealth you have is a measure of your success in life and of your worth as a person. The rich man is to be honoured, praised, admired and copied. Rich men are winners, the poor are losers. Sharp business practice is clever and acceptable. Greed is good.' Do you hear this kind of wisdom? These are powerful messages and affect our lives and choices.

But Proverbs teaches us a great lesson. The fear of the Lord, love, peace, and righteousness are true and lasting wealth. They are of much greater value than much money and wealth with turmoil, hatred, unrighteousness and injustice. Wisdom advises us:

> 'Don't wear yourself out trying to get rich; restrain yourself!
> Riches disappear in the blink of an eye;
> Wealth sprouts wings and flies off into the wild blue yonder.'

> (23:4-5 The Message)

THE WAY OF WISDOM IS NOT THE WAY OF POVERTY.

Wisdom makes us this promise:

> 'With me are riches and honour, enduring wealth and prosperity.
> My fruit is better than fine gold;
> What I yield surpasses choice silver.' (8:18-19).

The wise person makes choices on the basis that spiritual blessings are better than money and wealth. And they remember that money and wealth have no eternal value. But money and wealth can be used to honour the Lord and bless others. Proverbs teaches us that we honour the Lord by sharing with the poor. And Proverbs 3:5-10 tells us to honour the Lord by giving Him 'the first fruits of all our crops.' This was written to a farming community. But the same principle applies to Christians living in towns, who receive wages. We honour the Lord by giving Him the first of all we receive.

THE WISE HONOUR THE LORD WITH THEIR WEALTH

Proverbs gives us clear principles to follow in acquiring and using wealth. Following those principles promotes personal, family and national well-being.

THE WISE ARE PEOPLE OF INTEGRITY AND HONESTY

Have you seen the old-fashioned scales that used weights, large metal disks? Sometimes people used to make the weights smaller in order to cheat and to give a reduced measure. But Proverbs tells us that 'accurate weights are the LORD's delight!' The LORD delights in all that is righteous, just and honest.

HONESTY AND INTEGRITY ARE HALLMARKS OF CHRISTIAN BUSINESS PRACTICE

The Bible tells us much about the dangers of money and wealth for God's people. The big danger is for people to love money and wealth. And we can also put our trust in these things instead of the Lord. Another danger is that we become proud and think we have achieved things by ourselves. There are also the dangers of greed, discontent, and covetousness. I've heard it said of a certain rich man, 'He is a self-made man, and he worships his maker!'

MONEY AND WEALTH CAN STEAL:

- The love of our hearts
- The worship of our lives
- The commitment of our beings

Have you seen this happen to a Christian? Proverbs 30:7-9 gives us the prayer of a wise man concerning money and wealth. I have found this prayer a great blessing in my life. He asks the Lord to keep him from both poverty and riches. He asks the Lord for enough money and wealth for his needs.

THE WISE ASK THE LORD FOR ENOUGH MONEY AND WEALTH

Proverbs tells us where we may find true riches: 10:22, 'The blessing of the Lord makes rich, and He adds no sorrow with it.' (RSV).

In his commentary on this verse Derek Kidner says: 'Wealth unspoilt. The Hebrew adds an emphatic pronoun; "it makes rich" – i.e. nothing else does.'

Do you have true riches, true wealth?

STUDY 6

WISDOM REGARDING OUR SEXUAL NATURE

QUESTIONS

DAY 1 *Genesis 1:26-28, 31; 2:22-25.*
a) Find at least three things this creation record tells us about human sexuality.

Proverbs 2:16-19.
b) How is the adulteress described and what is the outcome of involvement with her?

DAY 2 *Proverbs 5:1-14 – Satan's Plan.*
a) What do we learn from the adulteress about those involved in immorality?

b) Does adultery pay what it promises? What is the reality?

DAY 3 *Proverbs 5:15-23 – God's Plan.*
a) What is God's plan for the expression of our sexual nature?

b) What does verse 19 reveal about the Lord and His plans for us?

c) What contrasts do you see between Satan's plan, verses 1-14 and God's plan, verses 15-23?

DAY 4 *Proverbs 6:23-35*
a) What helpful warnings and advice are we given to handle temptations to immorality?

b) How does verse 32 fit in with the wisdom of the world regarding sexual sin? How does it fit in with what Paul says in 1 Corinthians 6:18?

QUESTIONS (contd)

DAY 5   *Proverbs 7 – The Simpleton.*
a) What description is given of the young man and what big mistake did he make?

b) What do verses 22-26 tell us about the price he pays for a short time of pleasure?

DAY 6   *Proverbs 7 – The Seductress.*
a)   How is the woman described and what tactics does she use to entice and trap the young man?

b) In verse 18, what does she offer? Compare her offer with Folly's offer in 9:17.

DAY 7   *Proverbs 23:26-28.*
a) Why is the father's appeal of verse 26 appropriate before his teaching in verses 27-28?

b) What strikes you about the attitude of the adulteress and how does her statement sound familiar?

c) Why do we need these warnings in Proverbs about sexual sin over and over again?

NOTES

GOD'S PLAN IN CREATION

In Genesis God tells us that He made us male and female. Sexuality was part of His creation, part of being made in His image. God saw all that He had made and it was 'very good!' God laid down His plan for the expression of our sexuality: marriage between one man and one woman, an exclusive, lifelong, sexual union. The woman was God's gift to the man. He was delighted with her, a true companion. She is essentially like him, but different. God blessed the physical union of that first couple.

As with all of God's good gifts, He gives us guidelines for the use of His gifts. God's plan for the expression of our sexuality is for our good and blessing. Satan always has a counterfeit plan.

SATAN'S PLAN

His plan for the expression of our sexuality includes immorality, perversion, adultery, unfaithfulness, and going to the prostitute. He speaks with honeyed words and with the promise of love. His plan for the expression of our sexuality is for our pain and destruction. The warnings in Proverbs about following Satan's plan are graphic. Temptations to immorality come to everyone. Proverbs gives us much help in the handling of this temptation. The big issue is the heart decision we each make to follow God's plan in this matter. A huge way to keep out of sexual sin is not to play with it – to avoid the situations and people that would cause us temptation. You are in danger as soon as your thoughts wander in this fatal direction.

GOD'S PLAN – ENJOY THE WIFE OF YOUR YOUTH

Chapter 5 speaks of this part of God's plan. It uses the picture of a well in the courtyard of a house. Water was a precious commodity in Israel. The well in a courtyard was the source of cool, refreshing water to satisfy those in the house. In Proverbs this picture is used of marriage. The man is to drink water from his own well. Just as people do not waste water, so a man is not to waste his strength on other women. The water from his well is to be his alone, not to be shared with others.

God speaks openly about our sexual nature. There is no shame in the way God speaks. Proverbs 5:19: 'A loving doe, a graceful deer – let her breasts satisfy you always, may you ever be captivated by her love.'

This verse says for the husband to be captivated by his wife's love. 'Captivated' translates a Hebrew word meaning, 'to be fully satisfied,' expressing the sense of a man being drunk with alcohol. He is to be drunk with the pleasure of his wife's love. This is God speaking. He plans delight, joy and true satisfaction for his children in sexual pleasure.

BE EVER CAPTIVATED BY HER LOVE

Although Proverbs speaks of the adulterer as a woman, men also behave in similar ways. They charm and deceive and seduce women to commit sexual sin.

SATAN'S PLAN – IN THE END SHE IS BITTER AS GALL (5:4).

Kidner's comment is: 'Proverbs does not allow us to forget it, whether for warning or encouragement, since nothing can be judged by its first stages…Here it utterly reverses the promise: the delicious ends as the disgusting; the soothing, as the murderous.'

One thing about sexual sin is that it is mostly done in secret. But 5:21 tells us the truth that 'a man's ways are in full view of the Lord, and He examines all his paths!' Proverbs tell us the truth about the price we pay for all sexual sin.

THE TRUTH ABOUT ADULTERY:

Adultery is described as:

An ox to the slaughter
A deer stepping into a trap
A bird going into a net

The message of Proverbs regarding sexual sin is: Guard your heart and mind. Keep away from all temptation. Look past the pleasure to the 'chambers of death.'

Kidner's comment on 7:1-5: 'The best advice is useless against strong temptation unless it is thoroughly taken to heart and translated into habits. Concern for it is to be as sensitive as one's care for the pupil (apple) of the eye.'

WHAT ARE YOU GOING TO DO WITH THIS ADVICE?

The following is a prayer that you could use personally or could pass on to others for whom it may be appropriate:

'Father thank You that my body is the temple of the Holy Spirit. I want my body to be a clean and beautiful temple for You. I want my life to be pure. Help me to enjoy my sexual nature only in ways that please You. Warn me if ever I am in danger of sexual sin. I know You will do Your part; help me to do mine. May I glorify You in my body. In Jesus' Name I ask this.

STUDY 7

WISDOM FOR SUCCESSFUL LIVING

QUESTIONS

DAY 1

a) What is the wisdom of the world regarding alcohol? To what extent do you think alcohol is a problem in our society?

Proverbs 3:9-10; 9:1-2, 5.
b) From these Scriptures what insights do you get about wine itself?

DAY 2 *Proverbs 20:1; 21:17; 23:19-21.*

a) What teaching did the father give his son about the dangers of food and alcohol?

b) What is the position of the wise in regard to food and alcohol?

DAY 3 *Proverbs 23:29-35.*

a) How is the drunkard described and how does he see things?

b) What truth about alcohol do you see in verses 31-32?

c) What does verse 35 tell us about the way the drinker is deceived?

DAY 4 *Proverbs 31:1-7.*

a) What does King Lemuel's mother tell him about the dangers of drinking for a leader?

Isaiah 5:11-12.
b) What can alcohol in excess do to anyone?

QUESTIONS (contd)

DAY 5   *Ephesians 5:15-19.*
a) What is the approach of the wise Christian to drinking in excess?

b) What do you think people are looking for in drinking to excess?

c) What is to be the outcome of being filled with the Spirit?

DAY 6   *Proverbs 6:6-11; 26:14.*
a) How does the ant shame the sluggard?

Proverbs 10:26; 13:4; 15:19; 18:9; 19:15; 21:25; 26:13-16.
b) How is the sluggard's life described?

DAY 7   *Proverbs 22:13; 26:13-15.*
a) What do you think about the sluggard's excuses?

b) How does he rationalise his laziness?

Proverbs 24:30-34.
c) What do you think of the sluggard and his stewardship of all he had been given?

NOTES

Proverbs speaks of many different life issues. As we read last week the stern warnings about adultery, so this week we read warnings about two other matters: drinking alcohol and laziness. They are important areas in life and key matters for successful living.

Proverbs 20:1 speaks about 'being led astray by wine.' Instead of walking in good ways for our lives, alcohol can lead men and women into destructive ways. Christians can also be led astray and walk in Satan's ways. But wine was a part of what Wisdom served at her feast. Very often we have trouble handling God's good gift. Some people put their trust in it, others love and worship Mammon (wealth), and others covet, cheat and steal. So it is with the use of alcohol, a gift from God, but often totally abused.

The father in Proverbs gives his son instruction as to how to be wise in the use of alcohol: 23:19-20 'Listen, my son, and be wise, … do not join those who drink too much wine.'

The big message of Proverbs regarding alcohol is:

THE FOOL GETS DRUNK

In Proverbs 23 we read the classic picture of the drunk. He or she has woe, sorrow, strife, bruises and bloodshot eyes. Kidner comments, 'His imagination is as uncontrollable as his legs.' Proverbs 23 gives us a picture of the destruction of the mind, body, soul and spirit of the drinker. As with adultery, Proverbs does not allow us to forget the end of the matter. Here something that looked inviting and tasted smooth in the end poisons like a serpent.

ALCOHOL POISONS LIKE A VIPER

One of my friends was married to a renowned Christian neuro-physician who was doing research into brain disease. They had six children. He is a son of well-known Christian parents. In his late thirties he began to drink wine with other Christians socially. Quite quickly he slipped into heavy binge drinking of spirits, severe enough to do brain damage. He became addicted, an alcoholic. Many times one of his sons put him to bed. His marriage and family have now broken up.

It does not read like a profile of an alcoholic, but it is. Drinking any alcohol at all is often a problem for some Christians because of the devastation it causes in the lives of other people. For this reason some have made a pledge of total abstinence. Many Christians apply Romans 14:13 to this issue, 'Let us stop passing judgment on one another. Instead, make up your mind not to put any stumbling block or obstacle in your brother's way.'

Ephesians 5:15-19 gives us some clues as to why people drink to excess. They are wanting music in their hearts. They are looking for joy. But they will never find it in alcohol. The attitude of the wise is not to be drunk with wine, but to be filled with the Spirit. This is the way of true joy. We are told to make music in our hearts to the Lord, to sing psalms, hymns and spiritual songs to one another and to be thankful. If you are experiencing a lack of joy in your life, this is the answer.

The other life issue this week, laziness, is also associated with a lack of self-discipline and right choices. In Proverbs we are introduced to the sluggard, the lazy person. The sluggard likes to rest and sleep. Rest and sleep are good. But there is a time to rest and sleep and a time to work. The lazy person makes wrong choices – to rest and sleep when it is time to work.

Kidner's comment is, 'The sluggard in Proverbs is a figure of tragic comedy, with his sheer animal laziness, his preposterous excuses and his final helplessness.'

The sluggard is to learn a lesson from nature, from the ant. Have you ever learned a lesson for your life from nature? Be on your watch to learn this way! Look out this week to learn something you can share with your group.

THE SLUGGARD DOES NOT BEGIN THINGS, FINISH THINGS OR FACE THINGS

The sluggard has lots of excuses for not working. Though amusing and outrageous, he believes them. Some lazy people may even say, 'I am trusting the Lord to give me all I need.'

In Proverbs 24 we read a description of the sluggard's vineyard. It was full of weeds and the grapevines covered with thorns. The stone fence was broken down. The lazy person is not wise in what the Lord has placed in his care. Sluggards just sleep through life, wasting the good gifts God gives.

In Matthew 25 we read the story Jesus told of the servants who had been given talents to use. The servant who had been given one talent put the talent in the hole in the ground. In the day of giving account for the use of the talents his master said, 'You wicked, lazy servant!'

Something to remember: We are servants of Christ (1 Cor. 4:1).

STUDY 8

WISDOM ABOUT PRIDE AND ANGER

QUESTIONS

DAY 1 *Proverbs 6:16-19.*
a) How does the Lord feel about haughty, proud eyes?

b) Haughty eyes may seem a minor issue. But what attitudes of heart go along with haughty eyes?

Proverbs 8:12-13.
c) How does Wisdom feel about pride and arrogance?

d) What kinds of things are we proud of?

DAY 2 *Proverbs 30:11-14.*
a) List at least four ways pride and arrogance is shown in people's lives.

Proverbs 13:10 and 21:24.
b) What other effects does pride have on people's lives.

DAY 3 *Proverbs 15:33; 18:12; 29:23.*
a) What contrasts do you see between the proud and the humble?

Proverbs 22:4.
b) What connection do you see between humility and the fear of the Lord?

DAY 4 *Proverbs 3:33-34; 11:2; Psalm 25:9 and Psalm 149:4.*
a) What are the consequences of pride and the blessings of walking in humility? From Proverbs 11:2, how are you to walk if you want to get wisdom?

QUESTIONS (contd)

Proverbs 15:25; 16:5; 18-19.
b) What warnings does the Lord give us about pride and the proud of heart?

DAY 5 *Proverbs 14:29; 15:18; 17:27; 19:11.*
Read the verses in several versions of the Bible.
a) What do these verses tell us about two different ways of handling anger and the consequences?

b) What is the choice of the wise?

DAY 6 *Proverbs 14:17, 29; 19:19; 29:22.*
a) What do these verses tell us about being hot-tempered and the results in our lives?

Proverbs 12:16; 19:11: 29:11.
b) What contrasts are made between the wise and fools?

DAY 7 *Proverbs 25:28*
a) What picture is given to us of a person that lacks self-control?

Proverbs 16:32.
b) What comparisons are given in this verse? What does this verse say to you about patience and self-control?

NOTES

As well as sexual sin, Proverbs gives us very strong warnings about the sin of pride. The New Bible Dictionary says, 'Rebellious pride, which refuses to depend on God and be subject to Him, but attributes to self the honour due to Him, figures as the very root and essence of sin.' (p. 1027).

People are proud of all kinds of things such as: education, job, intelligence, possessions, family background, race, skills and abilities, beauty, position, strength, spiritual gifts, biblical knowledge and denomination. The list could go on and on.

I believe that many of us, sophisticated, modern Christians, do not take pride seriously. We have become numb to the seriousness of pride. Many of the advertisements on television feed our pride. Have you heard words in advertisements like: 'For the most important person in the world – You!' But Proverbs, along with the rest of Scripture, teaches this important truth: 'The LORD hates pride.'

THINK ABOUT WHAT PRIDE DOES IN OUR LIVES

Racial pride makes people feel superior and they despise others. Religious pride cuts people off from God's presence, from His grace and power. Pride stops us from being teachable. It stops us being corrected when we are wrong. Pride says, 'I am right!' Pride stops us having sorrow over sin. It stops us confessing our sin to the Lord. It stops us saying to others, 'I have sinned. Please forgive me.'

DO YOU AGREE THIS IS TRUE OF YOU?

As we have seen Proverbs never lets us forget THE END of matters. This is also true of pride. Proverbs gives each one of us this strong warning: Pride goes before destruction.

Maybe you have seen the outworking of 'pride comes before destruction,' in the demise of politicians, businessmen and tele-evangelists!

THE EVIL OF PRIDE IS THAT IT OPPOSES THE FEAR OF THE LORD

Proverbs urges us to choose to walk in the better way, that of humility. With humility comes wisdom, and also God gives grace to the humble – wonderful blessings!A proud heart or a humble heart? What is your choice.

Like so many things, it is a matter of choice. We see this also in the matter of anger. In his book, *Anger Is A Choice*, Tim La Haye addresses the issue of handling anger. He says 'the complex emotion' of anger is like every other emotion, God-given. So anger is everyone's problem. He writes: 'The truth of the matter is that anger in itself is neither good nor bad. It is just anger. It is an emotion. The problem is not the experience of feeling anger ... at first. The problem with anger is the direction in which it leads you. Or better stated, which direction you allow your anger to go.'

The wise are patient and slow to anger. But fools are quick-tempered, hot-tempered. Proverbs warns us of the outcome in our lives of being quick to anger. Proverbs tells us of the benefits and blessings of being slow to anger. Proverbs 29:11: 'A fool gives full vent to his anger, but a wise man keeps himself under control.'

On this verse, Derek Kidner says: 'Line 2 is literally, "but a wise man calms it back". If the verb indicates repression, the verb (used in the stilling of a storm) speaks of anger overcome, not merely checked.'

Proverbs 17:27: 'A man (or woman) of knowledge uses words with restraint, and a man of understanding is even-tempered.'

Being even-tempered is one of the ways we can bear a family likeness of our Heavenly Father. Numbers 14:8 tells us that 'The Lord is slow to anger.'

STUDY 9

WISDOM FOR FAMILY LIVING

QUESTIONS

DAY 1 *Proverbs 12:4; 31:10.*
(The root idea of the Hebrew word translated, 'noble character', is that of moral strength and worth. It also has the idea of practical efficiency).
a) What do these verses tell us about a fine wife?

Proverbs 9:1; 14:1.
b) What insights do you get about the work of a fine wife?

c) What can help build our homes, and what tears our homes down?

DAY 2 *Proverbs 31:10-31.*
a) In the following verses what qualities do you see in the life of the wife and what does she do?

Verses 13, 14-15, 16-18, 20, 21, 22, 24, 25, 26, 27.
b) What challenges you most about this woman? Is there an application you need to make to your life?

DAY 3 *Proverbs 31:10-31.*
a) From verses 11-12 and 28-29, how does her family feel about her?

Proverbs 11:22; 31:30.
b) What comment does Proverbs make on charm and beauty? What does Proverbs say is better?

DAY 4 *Proverbs 1:8-9; 3:1-2; 4:1-2; 6:20; 22:6.*
a) What thing of great value are parents to give their children?

QUESTIONS (contd)

Proverbs 3:1-2; 4:1-6; 7:1-2; 13:1.
b) What do we learn from the three generations in 4:1-6?

c) What outcome from the training were the parents desiring in their son's life?

DAY 5 *Proverbs 19: 18; 22:15.*
a) How does Proverbs see children?

Proverbs 13:24; 23:13-14; 29:15, 17.
b) Along with teaching what are wise and loving parents to do?

DAY 6 *Proverbs 3:27-29; 11:12; 24:28; 26:18-19.*
a) How are the wise to live with their neighbours?

Proverbs 17:17; 18:24; 27:9-10.
b) The wise are what kind of friends?

DAY 7 *Proverbs 27:5-6; 29:5.*
a) What do wise and loving friends do for each other?

b) Can you remember when a rebuke from a friend was a great blessing?

Proverbs 27:17.
c) Do you have friends that sharpen you when you are with them? What is it about them that sharpens you?

NOTES

This week we concentrate on what Proverbs says on wives, family living, children, friends and neighbours. As marriage and the family are God's plan for our living together, we may expect Proverbs has some important things to say to us. One of the themes of Proverbs is the very great value of a fine wife.

A PRUDENT WIFE IS FROM THE LORD (Prov. 19:14b)

Proverbs 18:22, 'He who finds a wife finds what is good and receives favour from the Lord.'Proverbs 8:35, 'Wisdom is speaking: For whoever finds me finds life and receives favour from the Lord.'

Derek Kidner says, 'These verses suggest that after wisdom itself, the best of God's blessings is a good wife.' Proverbs 31:10 makes a similar comparison, putting her price, like wisdom's (8:1), above rubies.

In the first verse of the poem in Proverbs 31 about the fine wife, we are asked, 'A wife of noble character who can find?'

In his book, *Reading Proverbs Today*, Graeme Goldsworthy says, 'This is not an impossible dream, but such a wife is sufficiently rare to require a diligent search.' In the first chapter of Proverbs we read, 'the fear of the Lord is the beginning of wisdom.' And in the last chapter there is the poem about the fine wife who fears the Lord. Proverbs 31:10-31 is an acrostic poem, each verse beginning with a successive letter of the Hebrew alphabet.

In summary we can say that Proverbs 31:10-31 is the practical application of wisdom and the fear of the Lord.

Ruth, the Moabite widow, in the Old Testament, is a good illustration of a fine wife. She feared the Lord and her life was a blessing to many. Just before she married her Jewish husband, Boaz, he said this to Ruth, 'All my fellow townsmen know that you are a woman of noble character,' (Ruth 3:11).

For those of us who are women this poem is a lovely example. And there is the challenge for each one of us to be worth far more than rubies! Throughout Proverbs we have the teaching of the parents for their son. The father appeals to his son, 'Listen to your father's instruction and do not forsake your mother's teaching.' These parents gave their children instruction, teaching,commands, sound learning, and words of insight. In his commentary Graeme Goldsworthy says, 'The terms, "instruction" and "teaching" indicate more than mere information giving; rather, the imparting of knowledge that is life – or character shaping.'

Parents work hard and sacrifice to give their children education, toys, holidays, music, dancing, good health care, good nutrition, fashionable clothes, a good home, sporting opportunities, job training and the list goes on. Some of these things have great value. But proverbs teaches us the thing of supreme value for our children's life and future is training in the way of the Lord. Are you like the parents in Proverbs?

Along with teaching and instruction, every child needs discipline. In Ephesians 6:1-3 and Colossians 3:20 we read the one thing God requires of children. They are to obey their parents. This pleases the Lord! In the home children need training in obedience. Children learn obedience so that they can obey the Lord as adults. Sometimes when discipline breaks down there is the need for punishment.

HE WHO SPARES THE ROD HATES HIS SON

In his book, *Dare to Discipline*, James Dobson has some helpful guidelines. He says that every act of disobedience is always to be punished. If done in love it never harms. But children do things that are part of being a child. They spill things, break things and are sometimes unable to meet demands. When parents punish for these things it makes the children angry and sad and is destructive.

The Lord plans that our lives should bless others, our friends and neighbours.

THE WISE ARE GOOD FRIENDS AND NEIGHBOURS

A good friend is faithful and loves through times of trouble and difficulty. Proverbs says, 'There is a friend who sticks closer than a brother.' This is the standard for being a good friend. The one who could do that perfectly was Jesus! But a lovely example of a friendship like this was between Jonathan, King Saul's son, and David, who had been anointed as the next king. Jonathan risked the wrath of his father in being a good friend to David. You can read about their friendship in 1 Samuel 18, 19.

Good friends love us enough to correct us in love, always for our good and blessing. As iron sharpens iron, so friends sharpen each other. We sharpen one another in many ways. Maybe it is by enthusiasm, quality of faith, confidence in God or assurance in prayer. I have some friends I appreciate very much. Their thinking, judgment, knowledge and spiritual insights sharpen me.

Kidner suggests that Proverbs teaches that these are four of the qualities of the wise friend: constancy, candour, counsel and tact.

Do you have a friend like this? Are you this kind of friend?

STUDY 10

WALKING IN WISDOM

QUESTIONS

DAY 1 *Proverbs 20:9; 15:11; 16:5; 19:3; 26:23-25; 28:14.*
a) What do these verses tell us about our hearts?

Proverbs 17:5, 9, 10, 17.
b) What heart attitudes are behind the behaviour described in these verses?

DAY 2 *Proverbs 4:20-23.*
a) Why is our heart, our inner person, so important to God?

b) What do you do to guard your heart?

Proverbs 2:2, 5; 3:1, 3.
c) What do you need to do to walk in wisdom, and what is the promise for those who apply their hearts to understanding?

DAY 3 *Proverbs 17:3.*
a) In the production of gold and silver, what is the purpose of the crucible and furnace? What insight does this give you as to the Lord's purpose in the testing of your heart?

Proverbs 27:21; John 12:42-43.
b) What do these verses tell us about praise being a test of our hearts?

DAY 4 *Proverbs 25:11-12; 15:31-33.*
a) What can be of great value in your life?

Proverbs 12:1, 15; 13:1, 10, 18; 15:12.
b) What is the attitude of the wise and of fools to correction?

QUESTIONS (contd)

DAY 5   *Isaiah 11:2.*
a) What did Isaiah prophesy about Jesus regarding wisdom?

Luke 2:39-40, 52; 4:16-23; Matthew 13:53-57.
b) How was Isaiah's prophecy fulfilled in Jesus?

DAY 6   *1 Corinthians 1:23-24; Colossians 2:1-3.*
a) What does Paul tell us about Jesus as regards wisdom?

b) What value have you found in studying Proverbs?

c) What truth came alive for you as you studied Proverbs?

DAY 7

a) What changes have there been in your attitudes and behaviour?

b) Write down one proverb that has impacted you.

Colossians 1:9-10.
c) Paul prayed that God would fill the Colossian Christians with the knowledge of His will through all spiritual wisdom and understanding. What was Paul's purpose in asking for this?

NOTES

As you have been reading Proverbs you would have noticed that this book has much to say about the heart. Proverbs teaches us that the attitudes of our hearts and the condition of our hearts are vital. Proverbs 4:23, 'Above all else, guard your heart, for it is the wellspring of life.'

The whole Bible emphasises the importance of the heart. Jesus told his disciples, 'Out of the heart comes evil thoughts, murder, adultery, sexual immorality, theft, false testimony, slander. These are what make a man (or woman) unclean.' (Matt. 15:19).

Proverbs teaches us that our hearts are sinful. Our hearts are not pure and clean in God's sight. Our hearts are arrogant and proud. Some people have hard hearts towards God. Others rage in their hearts against the Lord. Our hearts are deceitful. God wants to deal with our hearts. We have read some of the things the Lord tells us to do about our hearts. You memorised Proverbs 3:6, that you are to trust in the Lord with all your heart. You are to guard your heart. Proverbs 2:2 tells you to apply your heart to understanding.

Proverbs 2:5 is a promise for those who apply their hearts to understanding, ... 'You will understand the fear of the Lord and find the knowledge of God.'

Derek Kidner comments on this verse: 'With these two phrases, "the fear of the Lord" and "the knowledge of God" this verse, encompasses the two classic Old Testament terms for true religion – the poles of awe and intimacy.'

The father in Proverbs appealed to his son with these words: 'My son, give me your heart.'

Our Heavenly Father, appeals to each one of us in similar words: 'My child, give me your heart.'

Proverbs also teaches us that the Lord tests our hearts. He tests us in order for us to become aware of what is in our hearts. He tests us in all kinds of ways. Circumstances, sickness, death of someone very close to us, crises such as unemployment, small irritations and disappointments are some of the ways our hearts are tested.

Proverbs 17:3 says, 'The crucible for silver and the furnace for gold, but the Lord tests the heart.'

Think about Derek Kidner's helpful comment on this verse: 'The second line by itself would make God only an examiner; but the first line implies that His trials are constructive: not for finding a person out but for sorting him out. When things reveal their relative worth under 'fiery trial', it is our part (since we are not inert metal) to pick out, with Him, 'the precious from the worthless', for the benefit is not automatic.

THE LORD USES THE TESTING EXPERIENCES IN OUR LIVES NOT TO DESTROY BUT TO IMPROVE US!

The Lord wants to change our hearts in many ways. He wants to change our proud, stubborn, and wilful hearts to become humble, correctable and teachable.

LIKE GOLD, WISE CORRECTION IS SOMETHING OF GREAT VALUE

Jesus is our example for walking in wisdom. Seven hundred years before Jesus was born, Isaiah prophesied that the spirit of wisdom would rest upon Jesus. As He grew up, He grew in wisdom. Jesus would have learned the wisdom of Proverbs as a boy.

JESUS WALKED IN ALL THE WISDOM OF PROVERBS

Jesus is all the wisdom of Proverbs with skin on. In Jesus the man, we see how a wise man lives. In Jesus are hidden all the treasures of wisdom and knowledge.

JESUS IS THE WISDOM OF GOD

In His teaching and ministry, people were amazed at His wisdom. Jesus used proverbs and many wise sayings to help people understand and remember His teaching. He said things like, 'Do to others as you would have them do to you', and 'Give to Caesar what is Caesar's and to God what is God's.'

I pray that you have found great value and blessing in your life as you have done this study. I pray that there have been changes in your attitudes and behaviour. Above all I pray that you have grown in wisdom – that you have more skill in living life.

My prayer for you as we finish this study (you may like to pray this prayer for yourself and the others in your group):

Colossians 1:9-10:
'I ask God to fill you with the knowledge of His will through all spiritual wisdom and understanding. And I pray this in order that you may live a life worthy of the Lord and may please Him in every way: bearing fruit in every good work, growing in the knowledge of God.'

ANSWER GUIDE

The following pages contain an Answer Guide. It is recommended that answers to the questions be attempted before turning to this guide. It is only a guide and the answers given should not be treated as exhaustive.

GUIDE TO INTRODUCTORY STUDY

The section, 'What's your Proverb' is important to help us to begin to think proverbially.

It is important that each study group member reads through Proverbs over the next ten weeks.

If you have access to a copy of *The Message*, the Introduction to Proverbs is helpful, emphasising the very practical nature of this book.

Bibliography

Proverbs Derek Kidner Tyndale Old Testament Commentaries

Good News Bible (Week 4)

The Message Eugene H Peterson (Week 5)

The New Bible Dictionary (Week 8)

Anger is A Choice Tim La Haye (Week 8)

Reading Proverbs Today Graeme Goldsworthy (Week 9)

Dare to Discipline James Dobson (Week 9).

ANSWERS TO STUDY 1

WISDOM IS SKILL IN LIVING LIFE

DAY 1 a) The purpose of Proverbs is: getting wisdom and discipline; understanding words of insight; acquiring a disciplined and prudent life; doing what is right and just and fair; giving prudence to the simple; giving knowledge and discretion to the young; the wise to add to their learning; the discerning to get guidance; understanding sayings of the wise.

b) The outcome of the learning is to do what is right and just and fair, i.e. it is very practical – not just knowing but doing!

DAY 2 a) As directed.

b) The teaching of both parents – father and mother.

c) The father talks with his son. He addresses the issues. He teaches. He warns. He helps him to see that his peers offer gain, but in the end they receive great loss. What they are doing takes away their lives.

DAY 3 a) Solomon.

b) unnamed people, just called 'the wise.'

c) Agur, son of Jakeh, and King Lemuel.

DAY 4 a) Solomon asked God for wisdom and knowledge. He knew that God had made him King. The people were God's people and Solomon wanted the wisdom and knowledge in order to lead and govern the people. Verse 11 also tells us that Solomon had asked for his 'heart's desire.'

b) Wealth, riches, honour, power, victory, a long and healthy life, and many other things people usually want more than wisdom.

DAY 5 a) God gave him wisdom, what he had asked for. As well He gave wealth, riches, honour.

b) God says He gives wisdom, and is willing to give wisdom also to you.

DAY 6 a) She was not in a remote place. She was not hidden. She was where the people were. She was in very accessible places – in the public squares, at the head of noisy streets, at the gateways of the city where people were coming and going. Where she could be heard.

b) She was calling to the simple, the mockers, the fools. She offered a rebuke and (v. 25) advice. She had wanted to pour out her heart to them. They did not respond but rejected her, they hated knowledge and did not choose the fear of the Lord.

ANSWERS TO STUDY 1 (contd)

WISDOM IS SKILL IN LIVING LIFE

c) Today, many hate, scorn, ridicule and scoff at the things of God. They also do not choose the fear of the Lord.

DAY 7 a) The wise and fools.
The Lord hates a perverse man (a fool), but takes the wise into His confidence.
The Lord's curse is on the home of the wicked (fools) but blesses the home of the wise.
God mocks the mockers (fools), but gives grace to the humble.
Fools are held up to shame, the wise inherit honour.

b) The wise man: built on the rock. In the storm the house was secure. He heard Jesus' words and put them into practise.
The fool: built his house on the sand. In the storm the house fell and was wrecked. He heard Jesus' words and did not put them into practise.

ANSWERS TO STUDY 2

CHOOSE THE WAY OF WISDOM

DAY 1 a) Verse 2 understanding; verse 3 insight; verse 5 knowledge of God; verse 11 discretion; verse 16 knowledge and understanding.

     b) Blessings of getting wisdom: verse 5 To understand the fear of the Lord and the knowledge of God; verses 7-8 victory and protection; verse 9 understanding of what is right, fair, just – every good path. Protection, and being guarded from wicked men and women, and the adulteress. Help to keep in paths of righteousness.

DAY 2 a) True commitment involves life choices. Diligence, application and effort are required. We are to apply our hearts, to call out, to cry aloud, to search for wisdom as something very precious.

     b) Verse 8 God guards and protects the way of the faithful; verse 9 There are good paths; verses 12-13 The wicked leave the straight paths to walk in dark ways; verse 15 The wicked walk in crooked paths; verse 15 The wicked are devious in their ways; verse 19 The wicked do not enter the paths of life.

DAY 3 a) It is the beginning – the foundation of wisdom.

     b) Bad kinds of fears: getting sick, having accidents, death, other people, bad things happening to the family, Friday 13th, walking under ladders, cancer, and many other things. Such fears cripple our lives and take away our peace and joy.

     c) Helpful fears: snakes, spiders, speeding in the car, thieves, faulty electrical things, swimming in polluted water. These fears help us take care and are for our protection.

DAY 4 a) It produces great stability, safety and is a blessing for the children. It is a fountain of life, turning a person from the snares of death. It brings rest and contentment (19:23). Brings wealth and honour and praise.

     b) Fools do not choose to fear the Lord.

DAY 5 a) She claims her words are worthy and right (v. 6); (v. 7): just (v. 8); no crookedness or perversity; faultless (v. 9). The choice of wisdom is better than silver, gold and rubies. No other things are of greater value. She hates wickedness, evil, pride, arrogance, evil behaviour, perverse speech.

     b) Your answer.

DAY 6 a) God hates: haughty eyes, a lying tongue, hands that shed innocent blood, a heart that works out evil plans, fools quick to rush into evil, a false witness, someone who stirs up trouble between brothers, the thoughts of the wicked, the proud of heart. God loves the thoughts of the pure.

ANSWERS TO STUDY 2 (contd)

CHOOSE THE WAY OF WISDOM

b) The wise hate all kinds of sin.

DAY 7 a) The fear of the Lord helps us avoid evil. It gives us a future and a hope.

b) In all three examples the people do not have the fear of the Lord. They do not hate the sin in which they are involved.

ANSWERS TO STUDY 3

THE BLESSING OF GETTING WISDOM

DAY 1 a) Trust God totally. Do not lean on my own understanding and in all things acknowledge His Lordship.

b) There will be different answers. For me it means clear leading and directions.

c) We are to trust the Lord with all our hearts. We are to fear the Lord.
Fear involves right heart attitudes in the presence of the Lord – awe. As our Father we are to trust Him – His mercy and grace, power, provision and protection.

DAY 2 a) Verse 16 long life, riches and honour, verse 17 we walk in pleasant ways and know peace, verse 18 life and blessing, verse 23 safekeeping, verse 24, keeping from fear.

b) Personal answers. Ensure people also answer the 'Why?'

DAY 3 a) Protection from the ways of wicked men and women. Wisdom watches over the wise. Protects us from the words of the wicked, and from those who are devious. Protects from the adulteress, i.e., those who tempt us sexually.

b) There will be different answers e.g. at work, neighbours, leaders in local government, politicians, in the media, for some in their families.

DAY 4 a) Verse 22 God's wisdom guides us. It speaks to us, verse 23 like a lamp and a light showing the way, bringing correction and much warning of the consequences of sin.

b) His Wisdom protects me from the immoral man or woman.

DAY 5 a) She has built her house. Prepared meat and wine – good food and set the table. She sends out her maids with invitations. She invites all mankind – the simple, the foolish and the wise.

b) She offers a feast – 'Come, eat and drink my food!'

c) She requires us to leave our simple ways and walk in the way of understanding.

DAY 6 a) Folly is loud, undisciplined and without knowledge.

b) The invitations look to be the same. Appear to offer the same things.

c) She offers enjoyment of sin: verse 17, delicious experiences.

DAY 7 a) The Lord gives wisdom.

b) Verse 7 Wisdom is supreme, the most important thing to get in life.
Worth everything, I have to get it, I am to love, embrace and esteem wisdom.

PROVERBS • ANSWER GUIDE ·········

ANSWERS TO STUDY 4

GOD'S WISDOM ON THE TONGUE

DAY 1 a) **THE WISE:** a fountain of life, speak wisdom, show restraint in their speech, tongue is like choice silver – valuable words, speech nourishes many, speak words that are fitting.

THE FOOL: Violent speech, doesn't know when not to speak, lying, slander, many words – much talking, perverse speech.

b) Nourish by: teaching the Word of God. By words of: kindness, comfort, praise, wisdom, testimony, prophecy, encouragement, apology.

DAY 2 a) Power of the tongue: able to destroy others, words of gossip go deep within, has the power of life and death. Words are of very great value.

b) Words can be life for another. My words have the power to bring life to others or to bring death.

DAY 3 a) Allow people to answer personally.

b) Dean took the teacher's words to heart as the truth about his life, his potential, his ability to succeed in anything. He died in his capacity to try, to succeed. The words brought death to his confidence, ambition and to his self-worth.

DAY 4 a) WISE: Gentle answers. Their speech rescues others instead of destroying them, they commend knowledge, tongues bring healing, their lips promote instruction, speak pleasant words that satisfy and bring healing.

b) Wonderful thing: The tongue of the wise can bring healing.

c) Tongue used for healing by: sharing the good news of the gospel, speaking peace to troubled people, soothing rather than inflaming situations, encouraging, praising, affirming, by no negative destructive criticism.

DAY 5 a) God hates a lying tongue and a false witness that pours out lies.

b) Truthful lips last forever – only the truth is permanent. The Lord delights in truthful people.
Lies don't last. The Lord detests lying lips. The righteous hate what is false. A lying witness and all lying will be punished. A lying tongue hates the person about whom it lies. Flattery, a form of lying, brings ruin.

b) Anything that is not complete truth is lies, no matter what we call it.

DAY 6 a) A trustworthy person keeps confidences. People who repeat matters divide friends. A gossip betrays confidences.

ANSWERS TO STUDY 4 (contd)

GOD'S WISDOM ON THE TONGUE

b) A gossip is not to be trusted, often malicious, wants to create strife and pain. The wicked listen to gossip. Gossip is delicious, enjoyed – we have an appetite for gossip, it enters deeply into a person. Gossip fuels quarrels.

c) Avoid all gossips, never join in.

DAY 7 a) Nagging is agitating, annoying – like a dripping tap, destroying the peace and harmony in a home. Like any habit, own up if you do it, confess it as sin, repent, ask God's forgiveness, help and strength.
Choose not to nag.

b) Boasting – don't do it. Let others praise you.

ANSWERS TO STUDY 5

WISDOM ABOUT WEALTH

DAY 1 a) There is the wisdom of the world and the wisdom of God. The wisdom of the world is foolishness to God and is futile. We need to give up the wisdom of the world. Need to become a 'fool' before you become wise.

b) Media: Money and wealth will end all your troubles, bring true happiness. The first thing in life is to acquire as much as you can. Greed is good. The rich are winners, the poor are losers. Money and wealth mean power. The rich are to be honoured, admired, copied. Riches are an evaluation of your worth as a person. The measure of your money and wealth is a measure of your success in life.

DAY 2 a) A little money and wealth with the fear of the Lord is better than great wealth and turmoil. A little with love and peace is better than great money and wealth with hatred and strife. A little with righteousness is better than much money and wealth with injustice.

b) Fear of the Lord, love, peace, righteousness and justice, spiritual blessings, are of far greater value and are better choices than much money and wealth with trouble.

DAY 3 a) Dangers of: not realising the limitations of wealth – worthless in the day of wrath, and trusting in riches and falling. Riches are of no eternal value, do not remain, are transitory.

b) Fear of the Lord, love, peace, righteousness and justice, spiritual blessings, are of greater value and are better choices than much money and wealth with trouble.

c) Their life is like a house with rooms filled with paintings, china, gold, beautiful and rare things.

DAY 4 a) Kindness to the needy, sharing food with the poor. Promise of:
Blessing, the reward of the Lord, supply –to lack nothing.

b) There will be individual answers, may include: The working poor, the oppressed, the deprived, the addicted, deserted wives. Those in the third world.

DAY 5 a) Honour the Lord by giving him the first of all we get. If we do so there is the promise of supply of all we need.

b) In giving to God, faith in His supply for all our needs is tested. Giving to God acknowledges Him as Giver of all and the first of all we get belongs to Him.

ANSWERS TO STUDY 5 (contd)

WISDOM ABOUT WEALTH

DAY 6 a) Bribes are effective, people get whatever they want. Bribes pervert the course of justice, destroy a nation's stability.

       b) Honesty and integrity.

DAY 7 a) He asked for his daily bread. He did not ask for riches – he may become proud and disown the Lord. He did not ask for poverty – he may be tempted to steal and dishonour the Lord.

       b) The blessing of the Lord.

ANSWERS TO STUDY 6

WISDOM REGARDING OUR SEXUAL NATURE

DAY 1 a) See notes, 'God's Plan in Creation.'

b) She is unfaithful–a wayward wife. Faithless and rebellious – ignores God's covenant with Israel, including the seventh commandment 'You shall not commit adultery.' Seductive – uses seductive words. Involvement with her brings death.

DAY 2 a) Often the adulteress is charming – much sweet, smooth talk. Their ways are shifty and slippery.
(Although Proverbs speaks of 'the adulteress' men also charm and seduce and deceive women to commit sexual sin.)

b) Adultery looks like something sweet, but ends up as bitter as gall. Adultery appears attractive but brings ruin and death to body and soul.

DAY 3 a) It is to be between a man and his wife alone! The sexual union is to be unique, exclusive – not to be shared with any other (vv. 15, 17). God plans for blessing, delight, rejoicing, love, satisfaction.

b) God plans great delight and enjoyment of our sexual nature in a loving marriage.

c) Satan's Plan: bitterness, robbery, deceitful charm, death/hell.

God's plan: rejoicing, satisfaction, love, blessing.

DAY 4 a) Be careful of the smooth talk of an adulteress. Don't lust in your heart – guard your thoughts. Warnings: immorality always hurts and burns, is always self-destructive and brings shame and disgrace. It is always punished.
Arouses fury and anger in others involved, e.g., the wronged husband.

b) The wisdom of the world regards sexual sin as a normal, acceptable part of life – not self-destructive. Proverbs verse 32 agrees with Paul's statement that, 'he who sins sexually sins against his own body.'

DAY 5 a) The young man is simple, naïve, lacks judgment, needing wisdom.
He wandered into temptation – went at sunset (at the wrong time), down her street near her corner (the wrong place.) He did not stay away from temptation.

b) He is like an ox to the slaughter, a deer stepping into a trap, a bird going into a net – all going to their death. He pays with his life.

ANSWERS TO STUDY 6 (contd)

WISDOM REGARDING OUR SEXUAL NATURE

DAY 6 a) The seductress: has crafty intent, is dressed like a prostitute – to entice a man, is loud, defiant, restless – out on the street waiting to trap a young man, waiting like an animal for its prey. She is forward, grabs him and kisses him. She tells him her story – no one would know about it. Her lie is, 'You are just the person I have been looking for!'

      b) She offers her idea of love – stolen pleasure. It is what Folly offered, stolen, secret pleasure.

DAY 7 a) The young man needs a heart that is right, a heart attitude to follow purity and shun immorality. He needs a heart that sees immorality for what it is – ruthless and puts people into captivity.

      b) She is blasé about her sin. Her attitude reminds us of Eve's defence after eating the forbidden fruit in the Garden of Eden.

      c) The number of warnings is an indication of how destructive this sin is. Temptation to immorality is very powerful. We need constant reminders of the price and results of this sin.

ANSWERS TO STUDY 7

WISDOM FOR SUCCESSFUL LIVING

DAY 1 a) Often there is much pressure to drink, to be a part of a group. The world says drinking is desirable, pleasurable, acceptable – part of the good life.

b) Wine is part of the blessing of God – it was part of the food served at Wisdom's feast.

DAY 2 a) Drinking wine and beer produces mocking and brawling – anger and irrational behaviour. Drinking can lead people astray. To love food and wine, i.e. to love pleasure, to have these things as a major priority in life, leads to poverty in all kinds of ways.

b) The wise are not led astray by drink. They are not involved with others eating and drinking to excess. They do not eat or drink more than they need or is good for them.

DAY 3 a) The drunkard has woe, sorrow, strife, complaints, bruises, bloodshot eyes, unsteady legs and hallucinations. He sees strange, confusing things – not reality.

b) Wine looks good in the cup and tastes smooth but its effect can be deadly, like the bite of a snake.

c) The drinker thinks he is all right. All he wants is another drink. He is deceived by thinking it is the answer to his dilemma.

DAY 4 a) The danger for a leader drinking is to forget good government, justice and the care of the oppressed.

b) Alcohol can take over people's lives – drinking from early morning to late at night. People can then forget God's deeds, God's works, and have no respect for creation – spiritual deadness.

DAY 5 a) Paul says do not get drunk on wine, which leads to debauchery.

b) I think people look for joy, enjoyment, and relaxation.

c) The outcome – expressions of joy – speaking to one another in psalms, hymns and spiritual songs, music in the heart to the Lord, thanksgiving.

DAY 6 a) The ant knows when and how to work. It is willing to work, is self-motivated.

b) Proverbs 13:4: He craves but gets nothing – frustration. His life is like a path blocked with thorns – useless. He is close to destruction. His life is like a deep sleep – not alive to life. He refuses to work.

ANSWERS TO STUDY 7 (contd)

WISDOM FOR SUCCESSFUL LIVING

DAY 7 a) Personal.

b) Excuses are funny, not to do with reality. He may have convinced himself, but others aren't. He rationalises his laziness with his reasons for not working – he thinks his laziness is reasonable behaviour.

c) He was a useless steward of his land and resources, the wall was in ruins, leaving the vineyard unprotected. The vines were choked with thorns and weeds. He would get little in return for his vineyard and it goes on being destroyed.

ANSWERS TO STUDY 8

WISDOM ABOUT PRIDE AND ANGER

DAY 1 a) The Lord hates, detests haughty eyes.

b) Heart attitudes of pride, superiority, self-centredness, self-importance.

c) Wisdom hates pride and arrogance.

d) Things of which we are proud – see the second paragraph of the notes.

DAY 2 a) Pride and arrogance is shown: in those who do not honour their parents but curse them; in self-righteousness; in haughty, disdainful eyes; in brutality; in oppression of the poor and weak.

DAY 3 a) The proud: They know downfall. They are brought low.
The humble: They gain honour.

b) Humility and the fear of the Lord go hand in hand. Only a humble heart allows us to have the fear of the Lord.

DAY 4 a) Consequences of pride: God mocks (opposes) the proud. Disgrace. Blessings of humility: God gives grace to the humble. Wisdom: God guides the humble and teaches them His way. He crowns them with salvation. If I want wisdom I must walk in humility.

b) The Lord tears down the proud man's house. The Lord detests all the proud of heart. The proud face certain punishment.

DAY 5 a) People can be patient, even-tempered, slow to anger, have a cool spirit. A patient man calms a quarrel. With patience an offence is overlooked. Or people can be quick-tempered, hot-tempered, have a hasty temper. This stirs up dissension.

b) The wise choose to be patient, slow to anger, even-tempered.

DAY 6 a) A hot-tempered person: does foolish things; will pay a penalty for doing it; stirs up dissension; commits many sins.

b) The wise: overlook an insult; have patience; it is to their glory to overlook an offence; keep themselves and their anger under control.
Fools show their annoyance.

DAY 7 a) A person who lacks self-control is like a city with its walls all broken down – defenceless, open to the attack of an enemy.

b) A patient person, one who is not easily provoked, is better than a warrior. One who controls his temper is better than one who captures a city. Patience and self-control require effort and indicate internal strength.

ANSWERS TO STUDY 9

WISDOM FOR FAMILY LIVING

DAY 1 a) She is her husband's crown – precious and of great value. She is worth looking for and is more precious than rubies.

b) As Wisdom has built her house, so a wise woman builds her house.

c) Things that build homes: Faithful marriages, celebrations, shared experiences, family activities, prayer and Bible reading, family worship, etc.
Things that tear our homes down: Divorce, strife, quarrels, violence, each living separate lives, etc.

DAY 2 a) Verse 13 hardworking, verses 14-15 provides good food for her household, verses 16-18 discerning in business deals and works hard, verse 20 compassionate and caring – cares for the poor and needy, verse 21 cares for her family – they are well clothed, verse 22 cares for herself, verse 24 good business woman – sells what she makes, verse 25 strength and dignity, verse 26 wisdom and she has a wise tongue, faithful to teach God's ways in her home, verse 27 has overall care for her home – is diligent.

DAY 3 a) Her husband has full confidence in her – he trusts her in all kinds of ways in the household, especially with finances. He knows she brings good to his life and his home. Her husband and children praise and bless her. 'You are the best!'

b) We often think that the outward (charm and beauty) is desirable and to be praised in a woman. Proverbs teaches that discretion, right judgment is much more important.

DAY 4 a) Mother and father giving teaching, instruction, commands – directions for life, training.

b) The father was teaching his sons. When the father was a boy, only young, his father also had taught him wisdom. God's wisdom was taught to the next generation, in the home, by the parents.

c) The desired outcome in the son's life was: long life, prosperity, for his son to love and get wisdom and understanding, for the son to embrace the teaching.

DAY 5 a) in need of discipline. Children are foolish and need correction.

b) Be careful to discipline children, using 'the rod' – the physical punishment if needed. Do not leave children to go their own way. ('The rod' – (could) stress tenderness, not to punish in anger and as a part of the example the parent is setting, Proverbs 4:3-4,11).

ANSWERS TO STUDY 9 (contd)

WISDOM FOR SUCCESSFUL LIVING

DAY 6 a) Relationship with neighbours marked by kindness, generosity, living at peace and not deceiving.

b) A friend is loving at all times, especially in hard times, committed and loyal, gives good counsel.

DAY 7 a) A true friend sometimes brings a wound – a loving rebuke, correction – not flattery which destroys.

b) Personal.

c) Personal.

ANSWERS TO STUDY 10

WALKING IN WISDOM

DAY 1 a) Hearts are: not pure, unclean, sinful, open before the Lord – nothing is hidden from Him. The Lord hates the proud of heart. Some hearts rage against the Lord, are evil, can harbour deceit, are filled with abominations, are hard.

b) Verse 5 mean, perverse, vengeful heart.
Verse 9 loving reconciling heart, and another that enjoys division and party spirit.
Verse 19 a sensitive, correctable heart.
Verse 17 a loving, caring heart, faithful and supportive.

DAY 2 a) It is the wellspring of life.

b) Personal.

c) Apply my heart to understanding, keep God's commands in my heart, write His Word in my heart.
The Promise: You will understand the fear of the Lord and find the knowledge of God.

DAY 3 a) It is to melt, to refine – to sort out the impurities and remove that which makes the gold or silver of less value, beauty and usefulness.
The Lord means testing not to destroy but to improve us – by removing the impurities – the rubbish from our lives.

b) Praise can be a test of our hearts. Some early Christians did not confess their faith in Jesus publicly because they chose the praise of men rather than the praise of God. If we do this it affects how we live and the choices we make.

DAY 4 a) An apt word: the right word at the right time, a wise rebuke, a life-giving rebuke, correction.

b) THE WISE: Listen to advice, take advice, heed instruction.
FOOLS: Hate correction, their way seems right to them and so they see no need of any correction, don't listen to correction, ignore it, resent it.

DAY 5 a) Isaiah prophesied that Jesus would have the Spirit of wisdom and of understanding, the Spirit of counsel and of power, the Spirit of knowledge and of the fear of the Lord. And He would delight in the fear of the Lord.

b) As Jesus grew, He grew in wisdom, He was filled with wisdom. In His ministry people were amazed at His wisdom and His gracious words. In Nazareth they were puzzled about where He got the wisdom and the miraculous powers.

ANSWERS TO STUDY 10 (contd)

WALKING IN WISDOM

DAY 6 a) Jesus is the wisdom of God. In Him are hidden all the treasures of wisdom and knowledge.

      b) Personal.

      c) Personal.

DAY 7 a) Personal.

      b) Personal.

      c) In order that those Christians would live a life worthy of the Lord, pleasing Him in every way, bearing fruit in every good work and increasing in the knowledge of God.

THE WORD WORLDWIDE

We first heard of WORD WORLDWIDE over twenty years ago when Marie Dinnen, its founder, shared excitedly about the wonderful way ministry to a needy woman had exploded to touch many lives. It was great to see the Word of God being made central in the lives of thousands of men and women, then the life changing effects that resulted when they applied the Word into their circumstances. Over the years the vision for WORD WORLDWIDE has not dimmed in the hearts of those who are involved in this ministry. God is still at work through His Word and in today's self-seeking society, the Word is even more relevant to those who desire true meaning and purpose in life. WORD WORLDWIDE is a ministry of WEC International, an inter-denominational missionary society, whose sole purpose for existence is to see Christ known, loved and worshipped by all, particularly those who have yet to hear of His wonderful name. This ministry is a vital part of our work and we warmly recommend the WORD WORLDWIDE 'Geared for Growth' Bible studies to you. We know that as you study His Word you will be enriched in your personal walk with Christ. It is our hope that as you are blessed through these studies, you will find opportunities to help others find a personal relationship with Jesus. As a mission we would encourage you to work with us to make Christ known to the ends of the earth.

Stewart and Jean Moulds – British Directors, **WEC International**.

GEARED FOR GROWTH BIBLE STUDIES

You can obtain a full list of over

50 'Geared for Growth' studies

and

order online

at:

Our Website:

www.gearedforgrowth.co.uk

Further information can also be obtained from:
www.christianfocus.com

Find out more about WEC INTERNATIONAL at:
www.wec-int.org.uk or on Facebook

Christian Focus Publications

publishes books for all ages

Our mission statement –

STAYING FAITHFUL

In dependence upon God we seek to impact the world through literature faithful to His infallible Word, the Bible. Our aim is to ensure that the Lord Jesus Christ is presented as the only hope to obtain forgiveness of sin, live a useful life and look forward to heaven with Him.

REACHING OUT

Christ's last command requires us to reach out to our world with His gospel. We seek to help fulfil that by publishing books that point people towards Jesus and help them develop a Christ-like maturity. We aim to equip all levels of readers for life, work, ministry and mission.

Books in our adult range are published in three imprints.

Christian Focus contains popular works including biographies, commentaries, basic doctrine and Christian living. Our children's books are also published in this imprint.

Mentor focuses on books written at a level suitable for Bible College and seminary students, pastors, and other serious readers. The imprint includes commentaries, doctrinal studies, examination of current issues and church history.

Christian Heritage contains classic writings from the past.